The FEMALE ADVOCATE; A POEM.
Occasioned by Reading Mr. Duncombe's Feminead.

(1774)

MARY SCOTT

Introduction by
GAE HOLLADAY

Publication Number 224
WILLIAM ANDREWS CLARK MEMORIAL LIBRARY
University of California, Los Angeles
1984

109323

GENERAL EDITOR

 DAVID STUART RODES, *University of California, Los Angeles*

EDITORS

 CHARLES L. BATTEN, *University of California, Los Angeles*
 GEORGE ROBERT GUFFEY, *University of California, Los Angeles*
 MAXIMILLIAN E. NOVAK, *University of California, Los Angeles*
 NANCY MALIM SHEA, *William Andrews Clark Memorial Library*
 THOMAS WRIGHT, *William Andrews Clark Memorial Library*

ADVISORY EDITORS

 PAULA R. BACKSCHEIDER, *University of Rochester*
 RALPH COHEN, *University of Virginia*
 WILLIAM E. CONWAY, *William Andrews Clark Memorial Library*
 VINTON A. DEARING, *University of California, Los Angeles*
 PHILLIP HARTH, *University of Wisconsin, Madison*
 ROBERT D. HUME, *Pennsylvania State University*
 LOUIS A. LANDA, *Princeton University*
 EARL MINER, *Princeton University*
 JAMES SUTHERLAND, *University College, London*
 NORMAN J. W. THROWER, *William Andrews Clark Memorial Library*
 ROBERT VOSPER, *William Andrews Clark Memorial Library*
 JOHN M. WALLACE, *University of Chicago*

PUBLICATIONS MANAGER

 NANCY MALIM SHEA, *William Andrews Clark Memorial Library*

CORRESPONDING SECRETARY

 BEVERLY J. ONLEY, *William Andrews Clark Memorial Library*

Introduction ©1984 by The William Andrews Clark Memorial Library
University of California, Los Angeles
2520 Cimarron Street, Los Angeles, California 90018

Designed and printed by The Castle Press, Pasadena, California

INTRODUCTION

Twenty years after John Duncombe's celebration of "female merit" in his poem *The Feminiad* (1754), Mary Scott continued his theme with *The Female Advocate; A Poem. Occasioned by Reading Mr. Duncombe's Feminead* (1774).[1] Regretting "that it was only on a small number of Female Geniuses that Gentleman bestowed the wreath of Fame" (v), Scott expands the catalogue of some twenty-five "*British* nymphs" (line 49) honored in *The Feminiad*. While Duncombe's list traces female genius since "Charles's days" (line 108), beginning with "Orinda" (Katherine Philips), Scott recovers the remarkable women of the Renaissance. *The Female Advocate* then brings Duncombe's list to date by celebrating those women "whom he omitted, as well as those who have obliged the world with their literary productions, since the publication of his elegant Poem" (v), concluding with Scott's contemporary, Anna Letitia Barbauld.

Of Mary Scott's own life little is known except that she resided in Milbourne Port, Somerset, published several poems, and suffered "years of ill health," as she complains in the dedication (viii). Her poems indicate strong religious fervor, but she cannot be linked with the Hertford Quaker Scotts, John and Samuel, who visited Mrs. Montagu's parties, nor associated with the distinguished Scotts of Bath, George and Sarah (Lady Mary Wortley Montagu's sister). Nonetheless, our Miss Scott may have enjoyed literary contacts in Bath, for her long poem *Messiah* appeared in 1788 "for the Benefit of the General Hospital at Bath."[2] *Messiah*, which casts Christ as an epic hero suffering betrayal and "the torturing conflicts of a feeling heart," was credited with harmonious versification, but the *Monthly Review* (79 [1788]: 277) feared that Scott's "Muse will be deemed an heretical one." One imagines Mary Scott and many eighteenth-century poets like her, such as Maria Riddell, Elizabeth Ryves, Amelia Pickering, Jane Cave, and aspiring writers catalogued in *The Female Advocate*, enjoying a literary life among a small circle, composing poems for private circulation or subscription publication, contributing to miscellany volumes such as *The Flower-Piece* (1731) or *The Flowers of*

Parnassus (1736), overseeing editions of their own works, or contributing poems to one of many editions of *Poems by Eminent Ladies* (1755) or Dodsley's *Collection of Poems* (1748). Such were the scattered resources for publication precursory to the more complete 1825 feminist collection by Alexander Dyce, *Specimens of British Poetesses*.

The Female Advocate, though it treads but cautiously over convention, is an early feminist document defending the rights of women to explore and develop their minds beyond the domestic sphere and the "imitative arts" (vi). In the dedication (addressed to Anne Steele, the "Theodosia" of the poem, according to two handwritten additions to the dedication of the first edition, reprinted here [v, viii]), Scott describes with "the most fervent zeal" (v) the injustices that moved her to defend her sex against the "contracted" sentiments of men: "have they not prohibited us from cultivating an acquaintance with the sciences? Do they not regard the woman who suffers her faculties to rust in a state of listless indolence, with a more favourable eye, than her who engages in a dispassionate search after truth?" (vi). Not all women have a natural talent for literature or the leisure to pursue serious studies, but, Scott insists, all women ought "to employ, part at least of, their leisure-hours, in improving their minds in useful knowledge" (viii).

This last assertion appears deceivingly modest to us now. But education for eighteenth-century women—how much and to what end?—is important to consider as we read *The Female Advocate*, for the subject demanded serious consideration during the century bridging the now famous proposals made by Mary Astell and Mary Wollstonecraft. Traditional objections to female education center on the prejudice that learning plunders piety, disrupts domestic duties, and undermines modesty.[3] Women's defenses, then, attempt to abate these fears. They demonstrate that education raises the merit and usefulness of women in virtue, domestic "oeconomy," and fruitful occupation of free time in study and conversation.

That female education initially had a specifically religious end is a point not to be overlooked.[4] Bathsua Makin, in the early defense *An Essay to Revive the Antient Education of Gentlewomen* (1673), takes no risk of being mistaken in her intent: "If any think all this Learning is but meerly humane, I acknowledge the great end of Arts and Tongues is the better to enable us to know God in Jesus Christ, and our own selves, that we may glorifie and enjoy him for ever" (15). The spiritual advantages of education are primary to Mary Astell's *A Serious Proposal* (1694), in which she asserts that serious discourse should be "Not the Follies of the Town, but the Beauties and Love of JESUS" (145); and studies of principles of religion and the Holy Scriptures occupy the first three chapters of Hester Chapone's *Letters* (1773). Far from corrupting women's religiosity, the feminists argued, learning nurtures Christian principle and behavior. Even the revolutionary pamphleteer "Sophia" proves that "*Virtue* and *Felicity* are equally requisite in a private, as well as in a public station, and *learning* is a necessary means to both" (27). Without "Sense," Lady Mary Wortley Montagu warns, "there can be no Virtue" (28).

Raising one's moral character should be the fruit of all learning for women—on this the eighteenth-century female advocates agreed. Acting on strict interpretation of this principle, the good reverend John Duncombe banishes from the ranks of the illustrious British fair the "wanton Muse" of Delarivière Manley, Susanna Centlivre, Aphra Behn, and three memoirists, "Virtue's female foes" (lines 148, 140). Virtue and studies are properly associated in Scott's poem, but the priority is clear: "Still next to virtue, science charms my eye" (line 517), and her eye is to Heaven, "For sure alone in Virtue can ye find, / Enjoyments suited to th'immortal mind" (lines 251-52). Mary Masters possesses, in Scott's encomium, "A mind with virtue, and with genius bless'd" (line 226); and Elizabeth Tollett's attainments in language, history, astronomy, and mathematics, Scott notes, "were crowned with the most fervent piety, and every moral virtue" (23n.).

Virtue is the primary issue. Domesticity nearly rivals it in importance. To overcome husbands' apprehensions of discovering "The prudent housewife in the scholar lost" (*The Feminiad*, line 85), arguments favoring education for women, such as Eliza Haywood's, assure that intellectual improvements "will never be of Prejudice to our attending to those lower Occupations of Life, which are not to be dispensed with except in those of the great World.—They will rather, by making a Woman more sensible than she could otherwise be, . . . [make her] doubly industrious" (Mahl and Koon, 234). Such reasoning invites the unenlightened to see household management and the instruction of servants and children as thoughtful arts rather than mundane tasks. Comprehension of mathematics, penetration of character through wide reading, and an understanding of the foundations of liberal knowledge, the argument went, improved a woman's domestic performance; it never exempted her from it. Even unmarried or childless learned women, such as Elizabeth Carter, Catherine Talbot, Maria Edgeworth, Anna Letitia Barbauld, and Hannah More fulfilled exemplary domestic lives.[5] More complains that it is not the truly learned women but the "smatterers" who bring discredit to the sex by "despising the duties of ordinary life" (ibid., 288). Scott, in a note to her poem, praises the modesty of Constantia Grierson, adding "nor did her attainments in literature, render her neglectful of the humbler duties of domestic life" (16n.).

Study, furthermore, drives away "Cards, Dice, Playes, and frothy Romances," Makin points out (26), and writers on education to follow her are pleased to display the improvements in conversation that result from female learning. The simple inquiry that inspired one of the first feminist tracts, Judith Drake's *An Essay In Defence of the Female Sex* (1696), was "whether the time an ingenious Gentleman spends in the Company of Women, may justly be said to be misemploy'd, or not? . . . Our Company is generally by our Adversaries represented as unprofitable and irksome to Men of Sense, and by some of the more vehement Sticklers against us, as Criminal." Whatever vices may be found in women, Drake concludes, "have in general both their source, and encouragement" from men (6, 8). Defenders of the sex agree that criticism of women for displaying empty minds amounts to hypocritical cant by those who disallow liberal educations for daughters and wives.

Typical of the literary protest against imprisonment by ignorance is Melissa's pointed reply to her well-named foils—Sir John Brute and Sir William Loveall—and to a Parson in Lady Mary Chudleigh's lively poetical tract, *The Ladies Defence* (1701):

> 'Tis hard we should be by the Men despis'd
> Yet kept from knowing what wou'd make us priz'd:
> Debarr'd from Knowledge, banish'd from the Schools,
> And with the utmost Industry bred Fools. (14)

Scott is clearly writing within an established, if minority, feminist position as she builds to the didactic climax of *The Female Advo-*

cate, launching a general defense of broad education for women (lines 437-64), disclaiming Salic law, and defying man's pride in thinking the throne of knowledge his own. Future years hold for women the promise of shared genius with men in science, divinity, history, poetry, physics, and natural history: "Alike in nature, arts, and manners read, / In ev'ry path of knowledge, see they tread!" (lines 461-62).

The condescending response of the *Monthly Review* to this visionary generation of female geniuses reminds us that such equality is still in process even two hundred years later. According to the reviewer, Scott very wrongmindedly hints that "this was the aera of their approaching liberty":

> . . . the ladies can never hope, in any considerable numbers, either to rival the men in literary fame, or to render themselves such rational, entertaining, and improving companions, as to reconcile us to their learning, till some persons of real and extensive knowledge introduce considerable improvements into their education.[6]

So stood majority opinion. But advocates for women's education since the seventeenth century made an impressive attempt to answer the unjust tirades against women for their silliness.

Still, the fact of widespread—to say nothing of equal— education for women lags forever behind the theory. Makin, even in 1673, creates catalogues of great women accomplished in tongues, linguistics, oration, logic, philosophy, mathematics, divinity, and poetry. "Sophia" goes so far as to demand "Equality of Power, Dignity, and Esteem" in such areas as public office, teaching capacities in science, and some military duties. Utopian visions for women's intellectual communities are evoked in the 1770s by the fertile imagination of Lady Mary Hamilton. Female characters in her novels speak knowledgeably of Newtonian philosophy, Italian architecture, classical and contemporary writers; they compose operas and in their epistles draw on images from chemistry.[7] Even the most enlightened eighteenth-century women ("Sophia" excepted) are content to remain in subjection where public careers in politics and government are concerned, having no desire for the accompanying risks of fatigue, danger, and crime. But education for religious, social, and personal enhancement, they argued, should go far beyond the standard curriculum of "Accomplishments" in music, dance, and drawing, with light reading in history and geography thrown in between French lessons and needlework. "I think it the highest Injustice," Lady Mary Wortley Montagu protests, "to be debarr'd the Entertainment of my Closet, and that the same Studies which raise the character of a Man should hurt that of a Woman."[8]

The Female Advocate, like *The Feminiad,* comprises not just a list, but a miniature biographical catalogue of notable women, a genre long exploited by moralists and feminists. The eighteenth century's fascination with diverse forms of biography, including grouped biographies concentrating on a single theme (such as female worthies) is well documented.[9] Biographical and moralistic material in the text and notes of *The Female Advocate* accommodates the public's increasing demand for biographical information of all varieties. At the same time that *The Female Advocate* fulfills Scott's feminist desire to disabuse the notion that women are unfit for learning, it also fulfills the conservative didactic function of biography to help the reader imitate virtue. Two themes of the poem—virtue and learning—are therefore integrated in the use of grouped biography for poetical expression in *The Female Advocate.* George Ballard's *Memoirs of Several Ladies of Great Britain* (Oxford, 1752), a source and model for Duncombe and Scott, is among the better-known collections of the British fair. *Biographium Faemineum, The Female Worthies: or, Memoirs of the most Illustrious Ladies of all Ages and Nations* (2 vols., 1766), published just eight years before *The Female Advocate,* provides further evidence of the contemporary interest in specialized biography and of growing curiosity about women's place in history. These two respectable biographical works were predated, however, by variously more eccentric catalogues of great women.

Among the more interesting seventeenth-century catalogues of women are those that employ biographical sketches of women in Scripture, legend, and history who demonstrate valor, constancy, martyrdom, piety, or learning. James Strong's *Joanereidos: or, Feminine Valour* (1645) offers a rather exceptional collection of "*Westerne* Amazons" (13). More characteristic is Charles Gerbier's *Elogium Heroinum: or, The Praise of Worthy Women* (1651), a survey comprehending Nicaula, Queen of Saba (who debated with Solomon); Themistoclea and Policrata (sister and daughter to Pythagoras); Plato's disciples Laschenea and Axiothia; the familiar nine Muses and twelve sybils; and many entries repeated in

The Female Advocate, including the Countess of Pembroke and the daughters of Sir Anthony Coke. "R. B." (Nathaniel Crouch) focuses on only nine women in Scripture and government (from Deborah, Judith, and Susanna to Andegona, princess of Spain) in his highly didactic collection of *Female Excellency* (1688). But John Shirley's ambitious work *The Illustrious History of Women* (1686) attempts in a broad survey of history employing lists of women in ten categories to "remove the Veile that obscured [Female perfection] from the Eyes of the Ignoranter part of the Masculine World" (preface). Here we find Sarah, Rachel, Leah, and Ruth in Holy Writ; Tabiola, Constantia, Zenobia, and Amasia discoursing theology; the Muses; and "that Phoenix of Virtue" (82) who seems to be included in every catalogue, Lady Jane Grey.

Examples of learned women ancient and modern are called up for Theophilus Dorrington's feminist argument in *The Excellent Woman Described* (1692) that women be taught—instead of "Useless Trifles"—physick, chirurgery, morality, languages, reasoning, and philosophy (preface, vi). By the end of the seventeenth century so predictable was the list of examples in defenses of women that Misogynes, the woman-hater in William Walsh's *A Dialogue Concerning Women* (1691) has great fun satirizing the convention: "Do not . . . fetch me a *Sappho* out of *Greece*; a *Cornelia,* the Mother of the *Gracchi,* out of *Rome*; an *Anna Maria Schurman* out of *Holland*; and think that in shewing me three Learned Women in three thousand years, you have gain'd your point; and from some few particular Instances, prov'd a general Conclusion" (32). Early biographical dictionaries include women,[10] and female *exempla* ornament such odd volumes as Madeleine de Scudéry's *The Female Orators* (1714); Josiah Martin's *A Vindication of Women's Preaching* (1717); and Thomas Amory's uncompleted *Memoirs of several ladies of Great Britain* (1755), intended to memorialize Unitarian women. Mary Scott suffered no shortage of reference materials to compose a list of fifty notable and learned females.

Clearly, it is a misconception to think of the turn of the nineteenth century as marking the first feminist demands for educational and personal improvement. Scott's panegyrical catalogue of Britain's "bright daughters" (line 25) occupies a significant—if only moderately progressive—middle position representing the feminist rumblings that men and women of "sense and learning" were already making. As her poem and the works preceding it demonstrate, there is already much for women to boast about and to hope for in the eighteenth century. Twisting the omnipresent reminder that women have been corrupt since Eve, Lady Mary Wortley Montagu remarked, "'Tis true the first Lady had so little experience that she hearken'd to the persuasions of an Impertinent Dangler; and if you mind the story, he succeeded by persuadeing her that she was not so wise as she should be, and I own I suspect something like this device under the raillerys that are so freely apply'd to the Fair Sex" (133). It would become harder and harder to succeed with such devices in the decades following *The Female Advocate*.

University of California
Santa Barbara

NOTES TO THE INTRODUCTION

1. *The Female Advocate* was reissued with a new title page in 1775. Its publisher, Joseph Johnson, well known for his adventurous association with liberal causes, published soon afterwards *Laws Respecting Women as they Regard their Natural Rights* (1777) and, later on, works by feminist Mary Wollstonecraft, novelist Mary Hays, and educational writers Maria Edgeworth and Anna Letitia Barbauld. See Gerald P. Tyson, *Joseph Johnson: A Liberal Publisher* (Iowa City: University of Iowa Press, 1979). *The Feminiad. A Poem* is reprinted in ARS 207 (1981); page references in the text are to this edition. The spelling *Feminead* in Scott's title suggests that she was using the second edition of Duncombe's poem, *The Feminead: Or, Female Genius. A Poem* (1757).

2. Two more poems by a Miss Scott appear in the fourth edition of *Poems by the Most Eminent Ladies of Great Britain and Ireland*, 2 vols. (1780): "Dunnotter Castle" and "Verses, On a Day of Prayer, for Success in War" (2:171-77). Their content and versification suggest that they were composed by Mary Scott.

3. Paula L. Barbour points out that satirists during the reign of James I "revived all the old arguments against education for women, some reverting to the pre-Vives idea that learning unsettles women and makes

them prideful and wicked" (introd. to Bathsua Makin, *An Essay to Revive the Antient Education of Gentlewomen* [1673], ARS 202 [1980], vi). See also *Satires on Women*, ARS 180 (1976). For an excellent summary of the traditional satirical pairing of learning and immorality in women, see Felicity A. Nussbaum, "Pope's 'To a Lady' and the Eighteenth-Century Woman," *Philological Quarterly* 54 (spring 1975): 444-56.

4. My discussion draws on the following educational writings by women; page or line references are to these editions: Bathsua Makin (see note 3); Mary Astell, *A Serious Proposal To the Ladies* (1694); Judith Drake, *An Essay In Defence of the Female Sex* (1696); Lady Mary Wortley Montagu, *The Nonsense of Common-Sense*, no. 6 (24 January 1738) in *Essays and Poems and Simplicity, a Comedy*, ed. Robert Halsband and Isobel Grundy (Oxford: Clarendon Press, 1977); "Sophia," *Woman Not Inferior to Man* (1739); Eliza Haywood, *The Female Spectator*, 4 vols. (1746), selections reprinted in *The Female Spectator: English Women Writers before 1800*, ed. Mary R. Mahl and Helene Koon (Bloomington: Indiana University Press; Old Westbury, N.Y.: Feminist Press, 1977); Mary Masters, *Familiar Letters and Poems on Several Occasions* (1755); Hester Chapone, *Letters on the Improvement of the Mind*, 2 vols. (1773); Laetitia Matilda Hawkins, *Letters on the Female Mind* (1793); Anna Letitia Barbauld, *On Female Studies*, selections from *Works* (1825), reprinted in Mahl and Koon; Hannah More, *The Practical Use of Female Knowledge*, selections from *Strictures on the Modern System of Female Education* (1799), reprinted in Mahl and Koon.

5. See Miriam Leranbaum, "'Mistresses of Orthodoxy': Education in the Lives and Writings of Late Eighteenth-Century English Women Writers," *Proceedings of the American Philosophical Society* 121, no. 4 (August 1977): 281-301.

6. To reinforce his position, the reviewer points to the current practice of schoolmistresses teaching "English Reading" in girls' boarding schools: "These oratorical masters, ignorant for the most part as their scholars, teach them to stamp and tear and mouth out of Shakespeare and Milton. The poor girls are thus rendered worse than ignorant; conceited without knowledge, and supercilious without taste. Hence the prejudices of the men, with respect to female learning, are by no means likely to be lessened" (51 [1774]: 389). The circular reasoning evident here, that female learning is discouraged and despised because there are no learned females to teach ignorant ones properly, is precisely the kind of injustice feminists were protesting.

7. The novels of Lady Mary Leslie Walker Hamilton are more campaigns for female education than they are interesting fiction. See *Letters from the Duchesse de Crui and others, on subjects moral and entertaining*

(1776), *Memoirs of the Marchioness de Louvoi* (1777), and *Munster Village* (1778).

8. Letter to Lady Bute, 10 October 1753, *The Complete Letters of Lady Mary Wortley Montagu*, 3 vols., ed. Robert Halsband (Oxford: Clarendon Press, 1967), 3:40.

9. Horace Walpole claims his grouping of royal and noble authors is no stranger than the odd volumes collecting specimens of mortals who have demonstrated a love of statues, died laughing, studied at Oxford, or proved illustrious bastards (*A Catalogue of the Royal and Noble Authors of England*, 2 vols. [Strawberry Hill, 1758], 1:ii-iii, quoted in Donald A. Stauffer, *The Art of Biography in Eighteenth-Century England*, 2 vols. [Princeton: Princeton University Press, 1941], 1:505). See Stauffer's discussion of eccentric grouped biography, 1:501-8.

10. For example, Edward Phillips's *Theatrum Poetarum* (1675) concludes with two appendixes, "Women Among the Antients Eminent for Poetry" (45 entries) and "Women Among the Moderns Eminent for Poetry" (25 entries). William Winstanley's *England's Worthies* (1684) also mentions a handful of women—those notable for martial spirits. Biographical volumes increasingly include the names of notable women already encountered in Ballard, Duncombe, and Scott. Treatment of female poets is consistently sympathetic, for example, in *The Lives of the Poets of Great Britain and Ireland . . . by Mr. Cibber*, 5 vols. (1753). Many names from *The Female Advocate* are standard entries by the end of the century when the enlarged edition of *A New and General Biographical Dictionary* (1798) appeared.

THE WOMEN OF *THE FEMALE ADVOCATE*

(An asterisk marks the names that Scott refers to only in the dedication or notes to the poem or that she groups under a family surname.)

Anna Letitia Aikin Barbauld (1743-1825), educational writer, editor.
Mary Barber (1690?-1757), minor poet.
Dorothea Mallet Celesia (1738-70), minor dramatist and poet.
"Celia," unidentified.
Mary Chandler (1687-1745), popular Bath poet.
*Hester Mulso Chapone (1727-1801), letter writer, essayist, influential educational theorist.

Mary, Lady Chudleigh (1656-1710), essayist in prose and verse.
Daughters of Sir Anthony Coke:
   *Mildred, Lady Burleigh (1526-89), linguist, learned lady.
   *Elizabeth, Lady Russel (b. ca. 1529), learned lady.
   *Katherine, Mrs. Killigrew (b. ca. 1530), linguist, poet, learned lady.
   *Margaret, Lady Rowlet (d. 1558), learned lady.
   *Anne, Lady Bacon (b. ca. 1527), translator, learned lady.
Elizabeth Cooper (fl. 1737), comic dramatist, literary anthologist.
Queen Elizabeth (1533-1603), scholar, letter writer, poet, translator.
Sarah Fielding (1710-68), novelist, educational writer, translator.
—— Greville (fl. 1770), minor poet.
*Lady Catherine Grey, afterwards Lady Seymour, Countess of Hertford (1538?-68), learned lady.
Lady Jane Grey (Lady Dudley) (1537-54), linguist, letter writer, devotional writer.
Constantia Grierson (1706?-33), naturally gifted linguist, editor of classics.
Elizabeth Griffith (1720?-93), comic dramatist, novelist, essayist, editor.
Mary Jones (fl. 1755), minor poet.
Anne Killigrew (1660-85), painter, poet.
A Lady (Poems by, 1771), Jael Henrietta Pye? (d. 1782), minor poet.
*A Lady (Poems by), unidentified.
A Lady (Sermons by), R. Roberts (fl. 1770), minor religious writer and translator.
Charlotte Ramsay Lennox (1730?-1804), novelist, translator.
Catherine Macaulay, afterwards Graham (1731-91), controversial historian.
Mary Masters (fl. 1755), minor poet.
"Miranda," the Hon. Mrs. Monk (d. ca. 1715), "natural genius," poet, translator.
Elizabeth Robinson Montagu (1720-1800), learned lady, letter writer, literary critic.
*Hannah More (1745-1833), prolific tract writer and essayist, novelist, influential educational theorist.
Daughters of Sir Thomas More:
   *Margaret Roper (1505?-44), linguist, treatise writer, learned lady.
   *Elizabeth Dancy (b. 1506?), learned lady.
   *Cecelia Heron (b. 1507?), learned lady.
Margaret Cavendish, Duchess of Newcastle (1623-73), biographer, miscellaneous essayist, poet.

"Orinda," Katherine Fowler Philips (1631-64), letter writer, translator, poet.

Queen Catherine Parr (1512-48), linguist, devotional prose writer.

*Mary Sidney Herbert, Countess of Pembroke (1561-1621), translator, editor, patron.

Sarah, Lady Pennington (fl. 1761), instructional writer.

*Laetitia Pilkington (1712-50), memoirist.

Rachel Wriothesley, Lady Russell (1636-1723), chronicler of life in letters.

Daughters of Edward Seymour, Duke of Somerset:
   *Lady Anne (d. 1588),   ⎫ composers of distichs
   *Lady Margaret (?),   ⎬ in honor of
   *Lady Jane (1541-61),   ⎭ Queen Margaret of Navarre.

Catherine Talbot (1721-70), esteemed moral and religious writer.

"Theodosia," Anne Steele (1717-78), minor devotional writer.

Elizabeth Tollett (1694-1754), minor poet, learned lady.

Mary Whateley, afterwards Darwell (fl. 1794), minor poet.

*Phillis Wheatley, afterwards Peters (1753?-84), Boston slave, devotional poet, memoirist.

Anna Williams (1706-83), minor prose writer and poet.

The Women of the 'Feminead' (1757); see ARS 207 (1981), introduction, xii.

BIBLIOGRAPHICAL NOTE

The Female Advocate (1774) is reproduced from the copy of the first edition in the Huntington Library (Shelf Mark: 437332). A typical type page (p. 7) measures 182 x 131 mm.

THE

FEMALE ADVOCATE;

A POEM.

Price Two Shillings.

THE FEMALE ADVOCATE;

A POEM.

OCCASIONED BY READING

Mr. DUNCOMBE's FEMINEAD.

> Self prais'd, *and grasping at despotic pow'r*,
> Man *looks on slav'ry as the female dow'r*;
> *To* nature's *boon ascribes what* force *has giv'n*,
> *And* usurpation *deems the gift of Heav'n*.
>
> ANONYMOUS.

By Miss SCOTT.

LONDON:
Printed for JOSEPH JOHNSON, No. 72, St. Paul's Church-Yard.
M.DCC.LXXIV.

T O

A L A D Y.

AS it was in compliance with my Dear Miſs ———'s *Steeles* requeſt this little Eſſay was finiſhed, to her alone can it now with propriety be inſcribed.

Mr. DUNCOMBE's Feminead you and I have often read with the moſt grateful pleaſure; and undoubtedly you remember, that we have alſo regretted that it was only on a ſmall number of Female Geniuſes that Gentleman beſtowed the wreath of Fame; and have wiſhed to ſee thoſe celebrated whom he omitted, as well as thoſe who have obliged the world with their literary productions, ſince the publication of his elegant Poem.

Being too well acquainted with the illiberal ſentiments of men in general in regard to our ſex, and prompted by the moſt fervent zeal for their privileges, I took up the pen with an intention of becoming their advocate; but thinking myſelf unequal to the taſk, it was quickly laid aſide, and probably never would have been reſumed,

sumed, had not your partiality to the Author led you to have been pleased with the specimen which you saw.

It may perhaps be objected that it was unnecessary to write on this subject, as the sentiments of all men of sense relative to female education are now more enlarged than they formerly were. I allow that they are so; but yet those of the generality (of men of sense and learning I mean, for it would be absurd to regard the opinions of those who are not such) are still very contracted. How much has been said, even by writers of distinguished reputation, of the distinction of sexes in souls, of the studies, and even of the virtues proper for women? If they have allowed us to study the imitative arts, have they not prohibited us from cultivating an acquaintance with the sciences? Do they not regard the woman who suffers her faculties to rust in a state of listless indolence, with a more favourable eye, than her who engages in a dispassionate search after truth? And is not an implicit acquiescence in the dictates of their understandings, esteemed by them as the sole criterion of good sense in a woman? I believe I am expressing myself with warmth, but I cannot help it; for when I speak, or write, on this subject, I feel an indignation which I cannot, and which indeed I do not wish to suppress: It has folly and cruelty for its objects, and therefore must be laudable; folly, because if there really are those advantages resulting from a liberal education which it is insinuated they have derived from thence, the wider

those

those advantages are diffused, the more will the happiness of society be promoted: And if the pleasures that flow from knowledge are of all others the most refined and permanent, it surely is extreme barbarity to endeavour to preclude us from enjoying them, when they allow our sensations to be far more exquisite than their own. But I flatter myself a time may come, when men will be as much ashamed to avow their narrow prejudices in regard to the abilities of our sex, as they are now fond to glory in them. A few such changes I have already seen; for facts have a powerful tendency to convince the understanding; and of late, Female Authors have appeared with honour, in almost every walk of literature. Several have started up since the writing of this little piece; the public favour has attested the merit of Mrs. Chapone's " Letters on the Im-" provement of the Mind;" and of Miss More's elegant Pastoral Drama, intituled, " A Search after Happiness." " Poems by Phillis Wheateley, a Negro Servant to Mr. " Wheateley of Boston;" and, "Poems by a Lady," printed for G. ROBINSON in Pater-noster-row, lately published, also possess considerable merit.

If I should be thought to have spoken with severity of men in general, I flatter myself I have not suffered one line to escape me, that can give pain to those of a more liberal turn of mind: For such, my heart feels all the esteem due to their exalted worth: They will approve of my design: And did they know how much, years of ill health have impaired every faculty of my mind, it might perhaps lead them to be favourable in their cenfures on the execution. My ear will I hope ever be attentive to the dictates of the candid Critic; but, I alfo hope I have fpirit enough to defpife the fneers of the narrow-minded Pedant.

But zealous as I really am in the caufe of my fex, yet I would not be underftood to infinuate that every woman is formed for literature: the greateft part of both fexes, are neceffarily confined to the bufinefs of life. All I contend for is, that it is a duty abfolutely incumbent on every woman whom nature hath bleft with talents, of what kind foever they may be, to improve them; and that that is much oftener the cafe than it is ufually fuppofed to be. As to thofe Ladies whofe fituation in life will not admit of their engaging very deep in literary refearches, it furely is commendable in them, to employ, part at leaft of, their leifure-hours, in improving their minds in ufeful knowledge: the advantages of an underftanding in any degree cultivated, are too obvious to need pointing out.

I am, with the fincereft regard,

My Dear Mifs *Steele*,

Your moft obliged friend,

Milborne Port,
May 10th, 1774.

MARY SCOTT.

THE

FEMALE ADVOCATE.

NOW, big with storms, rough winter issues forth
From the cold bosom of his parent North;
Now, scarce a flow'ret rears its beauteous head
Above the surface of its native bed;
Stripp'd of its foliage, the late verdant grove, 5
No more invites my devious feet to rove:
How shall I soothe the anguish of a heart,
Yet bleeding from affliction's poignant dart?

A heart that long, alas, hath ceas'd to glow,
Dead to each hope of happiness below! 10
Propitious come, ye fair AONIAN maids,
And guide a wanderer to your hallow'd shades;
O, wrap me in your solitary cells
Where Silence reigns, and Inspiration dwells!
For once this tasteless apathy controul, 15
And wake each sprightly passion of my soul.

But say what theme shall sportive Fancy chuse,
Since nature's charms no more delight the Muse?
What theme! and can it then a doubt remain
What theme demands the tributary strain, 20
Whilst LORDLY MAN asserts his right divine,
Alone to bow at wisdom's sacred shrine;
With tyrant sway would keep the female mind
In error's cheerless dark abyss confin'd?
Tell what bright daughters BRITAIN once could boast, 25
What daughters now adorn HER happy coast.

In ages paſt, when learning's feeble ray
Firſt ſhone prophetic of a brighter day,
The female boſom caught the ſacred flame,
And on her eagle-pinion ſoar'd to fame. 30
Emerging from the gloom of mental night,
Illuſtrious PARR* firſt roſe divinely bright,

* *Catherine Parr*, daughter of Sir *Thomas Parr* of *Kendall*, and the ſixth and laſt wife to King *Henry* VIII. She enjoyed the advantages of a liberal education, and was a woman of great ſenſe, ſingular prudence, and a moſt ſtrenuous friend to the reformation; which ſhe ſtudied to promote to the extent of her power. She frequently argued with the King on the ſubject of Religion, and urged him, as he had already ſeparated from the *See* of *Rome*, to accompliſh the glorious work he had begun; and thoroughly to refine the *Church* from the remains of ſuperſtition that ſtill contaminated it. Impatient as *Henry* was of controul, ſuch was his opinion of her worth, and ſuch the affection he bore to her perſon, that he ſeldom betrayed the leaſt indications of diſguſt at her freedom. She was very aſſiduous in ſtudying the *Sacred Writings*, and books of Divinity, and occaſionally had Sermons preached to herſelf, and ſuch of the ladies of her bed-chamber as choſe to be preſent, by ſeveral eminent Proteſtant divines, whom ſhe retained in the character of Chaplains: for ſhe dared to be the patroneſs of truth at a time when its profeſſors were expoſed to the utmoſt danger: After her death a diſcourſe of her's, found amongſt her papers, was publiſhed, intituled, Queen *Catharine Parr's Lamentations of a Sinner, bewailing the Ignorance of her blind Life.*

An inftrument in Heav'n's o'er-ruling hand,
To fuccour truth, and blefs a guilty land,
The rage of fuperftition to controul, 35
And chafe the mifts of error from the foul.

Next beauteous DUDLEY* rofe to grace the ftage,
The pride and wonder of her fex and age!
Low bending at the radiant fhrine of truth,
Her foul renounc'd the idle toys of youth: 40
Impell'd by nobler fires, fhe boldly foar'd,
And every fcience, every art explor'd:
Religion in its pureft form array'd,
Her tongue, her manners, and her pen † difplay'd.

---

* Lady *Jane Grey*, wife to Lord *Guildford Dudley*. Her virtues, learning, and fufferings, are fo well known, that it would be impertinent to particularize them.

† See her letter to Mr. *Harding*, her Father's Chaplain, after his renunciation of the Proteftant faith; and letters to her father and fifter, in the 3d vol. of Fox's Ecclefiaftical Hiftory.

Rais'd to the splendid burden of a crown, 45
But soon compell'd to lay that burden down,
Torn sudden from a husband, from a throne,
'Twas then the heroine, then the Christian shone!
Her steady soul fate's fiercest frown could brave,
Secure of lasting bliss beyond the grave! 50

   O Faith, whose sacred transports never cloy,
Sweet prelibation of immortal joy!
What proud Philosophy but aims to preach,
'Tis thine with energy divine to teach:
Inspir'd by thee, we learn to smile at pain, 55
And all the vanities of life disdain;
Can calmly meet the sudden stroke of fate,
Or wait, if Heav'n approves, a longer date;
Convinc'd, howe'er Eternal Truth decides,
A parent's love still o'er our weal presides. 60

And THOU, with nature's nobleft gifts endu'd,
(Whom rival Kings with eyes of envy view'd,)
ELIZA!* Britain's ever-fav'rite name,
How vain the Mufe's wifh to fpeak thy fame!

 Long, hid beneath the fpecious mafk of zeal,   65
Had bigot rage deftroy'd the public weal;
Red with the blood of martyr'd faints, the land
Implor'd relief from Heav'n's benignant hand:
Heav'n heard her cries, beheld her flowing tears,
And fent ELIZA to avert her fears;   70
Again, Religion rear'd her radiant head,
And all around her facred influence fpread.
To wifdom early train'd by adverfe fate,
ELIZA knew to guide the helm of ftate;
 Twas HER's to check the haughty power of Spain,   75
And faction ftrove againft her life in vain.
Studious by each endearing art to prove,
HER conduct worthy of HER peoples' love,

   * Queen Elizabeth.

Yet would SHE from those glorious cares descend,
And with the Muse * HER vacant moments spend : 80
Well spoke HER verse HER great undaunted soul,
Which, form'd for empire, scorn'd to brook controul.

MORES, SEYMOURS, COKES, † a bright assemblage shone,
And shar'd the palm man fondly thought his own.

---

* The ingenious Dr. Percy, in his *Reliques of antient English Poetry*, hath obliged the world with two or three Poems written by Queen Elizabeth.

† Three daughters of Sir *Thomas More, Margaret, Elizabeth* and *Cicely*; all women of great talents and learning : But *Margaret* (wife to Mr. *Roper* of *Eltham* in *Kent*) seems to have been the most distinguished. She was a perfect mistress of the *Greek* and *Latin* tongues. She wrote two Latin Orations; and a Treatise of the *Four Last Things*, with so much fervor of devotion, and strength of reasoning, that her father declared it to be a better performance, than a discourse of the same nature written by himself. She also well understood Musick and Mathematics, and was complimented by the greatest men of the age, on account of her learning and accomplishments. She had a daughter little inferior to herself in Genius and Learning, who translated into English part of a Latin work of her grandfather; and also *Eusebius's* Ecclesiastical History, out of *Greek* into *Latin*. See the Life of Sir *Thomas More* in the second vol. of *British Biography*.

See, bending o'er NEWCASTLE's * sacred urn,   85
The Muses sigh, and drooping Fancy mourn!

For Three daughters of *Edward Seymour* Duke of *Somerset*; uncle, and Protector of King *Edward* VI. who were also greatly celebrated for their learning and genius.

Five daughters of Sir *Anthony Coke*, tutor to King *Edward* VI. who were famous for their knowledge in the learned languages. *Ann* the eldest was married to Sir *Nicholas*, and mother of the great Lord *Bacon*. She translated Bishop Jewel's *Apology for the Church* of England out of *Latin* into *English*; and sent a copy of her translation to the Bishop for his perusal, accompanied with a letter written in Greek; who returned her an answer in the same language, and declared it was so correct, that it needed not the least amendment. It was published in 1564, by the particular direction of Archbishop *Parker*. See the life of Sir *Nicholas Bacon* in the third vol. of *British Biography*.

Among the above-mentioned illustrious ornaments of that age, may be ranked Lady *Catharine Grey*, sister to Lady *Jane Grey*, who is also said to have been a woman of considerable learning; and the Countess of *Pembroke*, sister to the famous Sir *Philip Sidney*: A woman of fine accomplishments, and a great patroness of polite literature.

How unfashionable soever such a maxim may be in our days, it seems to have been a received one by the ladies in that æra, *that virtue* and *learning were the greatest ornaments of a woman!*

* Margaret Dutchess of *Newcastle* was the youngest daughter of Sir *Charles Lucas*, and born in the reign of King *James* I. She is said to have dis-

For well SHE knew on vent'rous wing to foar,
And trace her fair ideal regions o'er.
O, had SHE liv'd in this more polifh'd age,
And judgment rein'd imagination's rage,   90
What magic fongs our raptur'd ears had bleft!
Our paffions rouz'd, or footh'd them all to reft.

In thee, illuftrious KILLEGREW, ‖ we find
The Poet's and the Painter's arts combin'd:

'Twas

covered even from her infancy a very ftrong propenfity to poetry and every kind of polite literature. The uncommon turn of many of her compofitions, fhews her to have been poffeffed of a luxuriant imagination. In 1643, fhe was made one of the Maids of Honour to *Henrietta*, confort to King *Charles* I. And when that Princefs left *England*, this Lady attended her to *France*; where fhe met with the Marquis of Newcaftle, to whom fhe was married during her refidence there. She died in 1673.

‖ Mrs. *Ann Killegrew*, daughter of *Henry Killegrew* (one of the Prebendaries of *Weftminfter*) was born a fhort time before the reftoration of King *Charles* II. Her naturally fine genius being improved by a polite education, fhe made a great proficiency in the kindred-arts of Poetry and Painting; efpecially in the latter, in which fhe probably might have rivalled the

C   greateft

'Twas thine, O all-accomplish'd maid, to charm 95
Each breast that Virtue, or that Wit could warm:
Though early lost to earth, thy favor'd name
In DRYDEN's verse shall boast immortal fame.
O dire disease! what havock hast thou made!
What crouds convey'd to death's impervious shade! 100
By thee our fair ORINDA * too expir'd,
Lov'd by the Muses, by the world admir'd!
(And thou, my CELIA, in life's gayest bloom
Felt'st its dread stroke, and met an early tomb:
Listless I touch the long-neglected lyre, 105
Now thy dear name has ceas'd my songs t' inspire.
No more shall Fancy's glowing page delight,
Or Art's proud trophies charm my aching sight,

greatest masters of her time, had not death arrested her in the bloom of youth and genius. She died of the small-pox, in the 25th year of her age. Her death was lamented in a long Ode by Mr. *Dryden*.

* The celebrated Mrs. *Catharine Phillips*, who also died of the small-pox.

Still the keen pangs of parting rend my breast,
And rob my days of peace, my nights of rest!) 110

Be RUSSELL's † name by ev'ry heart approv'd,
Whilst thou, celestial Piety, art lov'd:
In her the strongest fortitude combin'd
With all the graces of a female mind:
The noblest pattern of connubial love, 115
'Twas hers the dread extreme of grief to prove.
Yet still convinc'd that providence is just,
She made its arm her unabating trust;
Saw lenient mercy blend her cup of woe,
And deal out all her portion here below: 120
Forever conscious of her Heav'nly birth,
And dead to all the vanities of earth,

† Lady *Rachel Russell*, daughter of *Thomas Wriothesly* Earl of *Southampton*, and wife to *William* Lord *Russell*, who was beheaded in the reign of King *Charles* II. See her letters.

Impatient to attain a purer clime,
With pain her foul fuftain'd the load of time.
Yet Heav'n long fpar'd her life to blefs the age, 125
And now fhe charms another by her page.
O, may that page, where all the virtues fhine
And faith's ftrong ardors breathe in every line,
Rouze the lethargic, animate the weak
The fordid ties of fenfe and time to break; 130
Since ev'ry wifh that centers here below,
Muft end in difappointment, pain, or woe!
Yet is not man unbleft, nor Heav'n unkind,
True pleafure dwells with ev'ry virtuous mind!
How falfe the toy that oft affumes its name, 135
For which we hazard honour, health and fame!
Like the coquette, fhe on each wooer fmiles,
And charms his fancy by her foothing wiles;
His love obtain'd, his fond embrace fhe flies,
And meets with cold difdain his longing eyes. 140

Eternal

Eternal wisdom, with benignant zeal,
Closely unites our duty and our weal:
Hence, when we quit the Heav'n-directed way,
And through the beaten paths of folly stray,
Peace and contentment wing their hasty flight, 145
And leave the mind a stranger to delight;
Wild anarchy prevails; and dire despair,
With tyrant sway, the ruffled breast shall tear.

Well do MIRANDA's * all-harmonious lays
Demand the Poet's tributary bays, 150

* The honourable Mrs. *Monk*, daughter of Lord *Molesworth*, and wife to *George Monk* Esquire. So great was her capacity, that she acquired, without the assistance of a teacher, a perfect knowledge of the *Latin, Italian* and *Spanish* tongues: she translated several Poems of the best authors in those languages, and wrote many original pieces. She died about the year 1715; and on her death-bed at *Bath*, wrote a very pathetic epistle in verse to her husband in *London*. Soon after her decease her Poems were published under the Title of, " *Mi-* " *randa,* or Poems by a *Lady*.".

Who trod through learning's arduous paths alone,
And made the wit of foreign climes our own;
Bleſt by the Muſe in life, nor left in death,
Her panting boſom felt th'inſpiring breath;
Love nerv'd her hand (ſtill to its object true)   155
To bid the partner of her cares adieu,
To bid him dry his ſorrow-ſtreaming eyes,
And gratulate her journey to the ſkies!

'Twas thine O CHUDLEIGH * (name for ever dear
Whilſt wit and virtue claim the lay ſincere!)   160

Boldly

---

* Lady *Chudleigh* was the daughter of *Richard Lee* Eſquire, of *Winſlade* in the County of *Devon*, and wife to Sir *George Chudleigh*. She ſeems to hint in ſome of her writings that ſhe had not enjoyed the advantages of a liberal education; but her application to ſtudy, and great capacity, enabled her to make a conſiderable figure amongſt her contemporary writers. She wrote many poetical pieces which were then highly approved of, and was a zealous aſſerter of the *female right to literature*. In 1710, ſhe publiſhed a volume of Eſſays in Proſe and Verſe dedicated to the Princeſs *Sophia* of

Hanover,

Boldly t'affert great Nature's equal laws,
And plead thy helplefs injur'd fex's caufe :
For that, thy fame fhall undecaying bloom,
And flow'rs unfading grow around thy tomb.

But fay, HIBERNIA, can this humble verfe 165
Thy own CONSTANTIA's † various praife rehearfe ?
What though her fortune low, her birth obfcure,
Sprung from a race illiterate, rude and poor;

Hanover, Mother of King *George* I, who was fo well pleafed with her Ladyfhip's compliments, that in return fhe fent her a letter in her own hand-writing; a copy of which is inferted in Lady *Chudleigh's* Life in the Biographical Dictionary.

† Mrs. *Conftantine Grierfon* was born in the county of *Kilkenny* in *Ireland*. She was a perfect miftrefs of the *Hebrew*, *Greek*, *Latin*, and *French* languages; and was equally well acquainted with Hiftory, Divinity, Philofophy, and Mathematics. She wrote a Dedication of the *Dublin* Edition of *Tacitus* to Lord *Carteret:* to his fon fhe wrote a Greek Epigram. She alfo wrote many Poems in *Englifh*, but on thofe fhe fet fo little value, that there are none of them extant, except a few interfperfed amongft Mrs. *Barber's* Poems; and two Epiftles to Mrs. *Pilkington*, publifhed by that Lady, in her Memoirs of her own

To all th' emoluments of art unknown,
Yet Wit and Learning mark'd her for their own. 170
With wond'rous ease, her comprehensive mind
The various stores of knowledge all combin'd:
A mind by nature form'd with strictest care
To teach us what superior beings are.
Of ev'ry virtue, ev'ry grace possest, 175
Weary of earth, impatient to be blest,
Soon her glad spirit broke each feeble tye
That held her here an exile from the sky;

own Life. To her great accomplishments Mrs. *Grierson* united the most fervent piety, and extensive benevolence. Her wit was not tinctured with ill-nature, nor her learning sullied with pride: nor did her attainments in literature, render her neglectful of the humbler duties of domestic life. What makes her character the more remarkable is, that she had no assistance in acquiring the great fund of knowledge which she possessed, besides a few accidental instructions from a Clergyman, who resided in the Parish in which she lived. Her parents were in too low a station of life to be capable of affording her any advantages of education. Previous to her marriage she was obliged to submit to the drudgery of the needle, to procure herself a subsistence. Her short intervals of leisure, were the only opportunities she enjoyed for study. She died at the age of 27.

For

For there, there only, could her soul improve;
Such her exalted piety and love! 180
 Thrice glorious hour, when truth's unclouded ray
Bursts on the mind in all the blaze of day!
For O, what more than pompous trifles, all
Those things we purblind mortals science call!
In youth, when new-born spirits fire the breast, 185
Of health, and hope, and vanity possefs'd,
With vigorous steps the arduous road we trace,
But soon are wearied in the dubious chace:
Errors, on ev'ry side, beset us round,
And soon our anxious, searching minds confound. 190
Thrice glorious hour, when truth's unclouded ray
Bursts on the mind in all the blaze of day!
Thrice glorious hour, her ardent vot'ries cry,
And pant for life and immortality!

      D   And

And THOU, * HIBERNIA's other fav'rite name,   195
Shall'ſt with CONSTANTIA's ever join thy fame.
Thy merit well the charming angel knew,
And plac'd it in the faireſt point of view.
Immortaliz'd by her, ſay, can the Muſe
The well-meant tribute of her praiſe refuſe?   200
Thy verſe for nobleſt ends was ſtill deſign'd;
To form aright the tender infant mind;
Vice to diſrobe of ev'ry fair diſguiſe,
And paint bright virtue to our raptur'd eyes.
Thee SWIFT, and noble ORRERY approv'd,   205
And ev'ry friend to modeſt merit lov'd.

   Whate'er, in beauty, nature had deny'd
To thee, O CHANDLER, † ſhe in wit ſupply'd.

* Mrs. *Barber*, the wife of a reputable tradeſman in *Dublin*: a very ingenious Poeteſs, a woman of the moſt diſtinguiſhed virtue, and a particular friend of Mrs. *Grierſon's*.

† Mrs. *Chandler*, ſiſter to the celebrated diſſenting clergyman of that name. Her Poems, the principal of which is " A deſcription of *Bath*, inſcribed

No rosy cheek, no lip of Tyrian dye,
No polish'd forehead, nor the sparkling eye, 210
Taught senseless beaus to prostrate at thy shrine,
And hail their blooming idol all-divine:
But virtue reign'd triumphant in thy heart,
And thine was Poetry's delightful art.

To OXFORD next the Muse transported turns, 215
Where JONES ‡ with all a Poet's ardour burns;
JONES, in whose strains another POPE we view,
Her wit so keen, her sentiments so true.
Like him the charming maid, with skill refin'd,
Hath pierc'd the deep recesses of the mind; 220

to her Royal Highness the Princess *Amelia*, have passed through several editions.

‡ See Essays in prose and verse by Miss *Jones*. A reader of taste and candour will not, perhaps, scruple to acknowledge, that her Epistle on Patience, addressed to Lord *Masham*, and that on Desire, to the honorable Miss *Lovelace*, are worthy the pen of our celebrated *ethic Poet*.

The latent principles of action trac'd,
And Truth with Art's enchanting beauties grac'd.

Ingenious Masters, * well thy tuneful lays
May claim the tribute of the Muse's praise;
Whose soaring mind a parent's frown depress'd,   225
A mind with virtue, and with genius bless'd!
And yet, how sweetly-soothing in thy strains,
The Royal Bard of Palæstine complains!
Well too thou paint'st those envious critics pride
Who, fond to cavil, merit's charms would hide.   230
Superior to the labour'd songs of Art
The verse that flows spontaneous from the heart!

---

* Mrs. *Mary Masters*, a native of *Otley* near *Leeds* in *Yorkshire*. She herself informs us, that " her genius for poetry was always discountenanced by her parents; that her education rose no higher than the Spelling-book, and the Writing Master; and that, till her merit got the better of her fortune, she was shut out from all commerce with the more knowing and polite part of the world." The first volume of her Poems and Letters was published 1733; the second came out in 1755.

But yet more sweet, more finish'd far the line,
Where Art, and Nature, in fair union shine.

Thou † who did'st pierce the shades of gothic night, 235
And bring the first faint dawn of wit to light;
Who did'st the rude essays of genius save,
From dark oblivion's all-devouring grave;
To thee, fair patron of the Muses songs,
To thee each grateful Poet's praise belongs: 240
Praise, the sole boon a poet can bestow,
And the sole meed his arduous labours know.
Precarious meed! for oft alas, the bard
Finds Envy rob him of that sweet reward:
Her baneful touch his laurels soon destroys, 245
And blasts the harvest of his promis'd joys.

† See the *Muses Library*, a collection of antient English Poetry, from the times of *Edward* the Confessor, to the reign of *James* I; with an account of the Lives and Characters of the Writers; by Mrs. *Cooper*.

O, then, ye favor'd few! whom wit inspires,
Whom taste refines, or thirst of glory fires,
To nobler objects turn the dazzled eye,
Than Honour, Fame, or Fortune can supply: 250
For sure alone in Virtue can ye find,
Enjoyments suited to th'immortal mind.
With ardour then her sacred paths pursue;
There still new pleasures strike the raptur'd view:
Give to ambition there its utmost scope: 255
Thus shall your bliss surpass your brightest hope.

'Twas Fielding's ‡ talent, with ingenuous Art,
To trace the secret mazes of the Heart.
In language tun'd to please its infant thought,
The tender breast with prudent care she taught. 260

‡ Mrs. *Fielding*, sister to the late *Henry Fielding* Esquire, and author of "The Adventures of *David Simple*;" "Letters between the principal Characters in *David Simple*;" "The *Governess*, or, the *Female Academy*;" "The Lives of *Cleopatra* and *Octavia*;" and "of a translation, from the Greek, of Xenophon's Memorabilia of Socrates."

Nature

Nature to HER, her boldeſt pencil lent,
And bleſt HER with a mind of vaſt extent;
A mind, that nobly ſcorn'd each low deſire,
And glow'd with pure Religion's warmeſt fire.

High in the records of immortal fame 265
Stands, charming TOLLETT! * thy illuſtrious name:
Thee Science led to her ſequeſter'd bow'rs,
And deck'd thy mind with all her faireſt flow'rs:
The charms of verſe, of rapt'rous ſounds, are thine,
The pencil's magic, and the lore divine. 270

* Mrs. *Elizabeth Tollett*, daughter of *George Tollett* Eſquire, Commiſſioner of the Navy in the reigns of King *William* and Queen *Ann*. Her father obſerving her uncommon genius, gave her ſo excellent an education, that, beſides making a great proficiency in the *fine Arts*, ſhe ſpoke fluently and correctly the *Latin*, *Italian*, and *French* languages; and well underſtood Hiſtory, Aſtronomy, and Mathematics. Theſe attainments were crowned with the moſt fervent piety, and every moral virtue. The former part of her life was ſpent in the Tower of London, (but under what circumſtances her Biographer has not informed us); the latter at *Stratford* and *Weſtham*. She died in February 1754. Her Poems were publiſhed in 1755.

O LENOX,

O Lenox, † thou " in various nature wife !"
Proceed to paint our follies as they rife ;
Bid the coquette in blufhes hide her face,
Which affectation robs of every grace :
Bid virtue, to her generous purpofe true,   275
Prefs on, and keep perfection ftill in view.
Thus may fuccefs thy great defigns attend,
And fame, and fortune, fmile on virtue's friend !

For love, for wit, and fentiments refin'd,
(Another Sappho with a purer mind !)   280
Endu'd with ev'ry charm that boafts to pleafe,
Good-nature, foftnefs, fprightlinefs, and eafe ;

---

† Mrs. *Charlotte Lenox*, author of " Shakefpear illuftrated, with critical Remarks ; of " The *Sifter*, a Comedy ;" and of, " The *Female Quixote*." She has alfo tranflated (from the French) *Brumoy's* Greek Theatre.

Long may'ft thou, tuneful FRANCES, * be renown'd;
Thy life with honour, as with virtue crown'd.

When THEODOSIA ‡ tunes her Heav'n-taught lyre, 285
What bofom burns not with feraphic fire?
Sweet harmonift! in thy extatic lines
Virtue in all her native graces fhines:
There, each bright hope in tuneful numbers flows,
And there, fair faith! thy facred ardour glows: 290
There, refignation fmiles on care and pain,
And rapt'rous joy attunes the grateful ftrain.
O yet may Heav'n its healing aid extend,
And yet to health reftore my valued friend:
Long be it ere her gentle fpirit rife, 295
To fill fome glorious manfion in the fkies.

* See Letters between *Henry* and *Frances*. *Frances* (otherwife Mrs. *Griffiths*) befides her fhare in thofe ingenious and entertaining Letters, has tranflated from the French the writings of *Ninon de L'Enclos*, and written *Amana* a Dramatic Poem, and *A Wife in the Right*, a Comedy.

‡ See Poems on fubjects chiefly devotional, by *Theodofia*, in two volumes.

Mrs. Ann Steele of Broughton author of the poems signed Theodosia.

But hark! what softly-plaintive strains I hear!
How sweet they vibrate on my list'ning ear!
Sure Greville's ‖ Muse must ev'ry bosom please
That finds a charm in elegance or ease: 300
Hers were those nice sensations of the heart,
Whose magic pow'r can pain to joy impart;
A feeling " heart, that like the needle true,
" Turn'd at each touch, and turning trembled too!"

Daughter of Shenstone * hail! hail charming maid, 305
Well hath thy pen fair nature's charms display'd!
The hill, the grove, the flow'r-enamell'd lawn,
Shine in thy lays in brightest colours drawn:
Nor be thy praise confin'd to rural themes,
Or idly-musing Fancy's pleasing dreams; 310

‖ See Mrs. Greville's beautiful Ode to Indifference.
* See original Poems by Miss *Wheately.*

But still may contemplation † (guest divine!)
Expand thy breast, and prompt the flowing line.

But thou MACAULAY, ‡ say, canst thou excuse
The fond presumption of a youthful Muse?
A Muse, that, raptur'd with thy growing fame,   315
Wishes (at least) to celebrate thy name;
A name, to ev'ry son of freedom dear,
Which patriots yet unborn shall long revere.

O Liberty! Heav'n's noblest gift below,
Without thee life were but one scene of woe: 320
Beneath thy sway, in these auspicious isles,
Science erects her laurell'd head, and smiles;
Our great AUGUSTUS lives the friend of Arts,
And reigns unrivall'd in their vot'ries Hearts.

† This couplet alludes to a fine Poem of that Lady's, intituled, "The Pleasures of Contemplation."
‡ Mrs. Macaulay the Historian.

A softer theme now claims the Muse's praise, 325
She feels the pow'r of ANNA's * tuneful lays:
Nor fortune's frowns, nor blindness could controul
The noble rage of her aspiring soul.
When pensive o'er the tomb of GREY † she mourns,
Each heart the sympathetic sigh returns. 330
In poor FLORILLA's varying fate we view,
How vain the toys our eager hopes pursue:
Nor wealth, nor wit, nor beauty can impart
One tranquil moment to the anxious heart.
Virtue! thou only smooth'st the brow of woe, 335
And thou alone can'st lasting bliss bestow!
Whilst o'er life's various sea my bark shall glide,
Do thou a pilot at the helm preside:

* See Miscellanies in Prose and Verse by *Anna Williams*.

† *Stephen Grey*, F. R. S. and author of the present doctrine of electricity. Mrs. *Williams* informs us, that she was the person who first discover'd the emission of the electrical spark from the human body, as she was assisting Mr. *Grey* in some of his experiments. She has since suffered a total loss of sight.

When

When gathering clouds the changing skies o'ercast,
When rough the surge, and loud the furious blast; 340
Or when the Heav'ns shall smile serenely fair,
Each wave roll smooth, and mild each breath of air;
Teach her one steady, glorious course to steer,
Not rashly bold, nor yet restrain'd by fear;
And may thy faithful compass guide her way, 345
To the bright regions of Eternal Day!

What various pow'rs in PENNINGTON * we find!
Taste, spirit, learning, elegance combin'd.
All-musing now in Contemplation's shades,
Her search the intellectual world pervades: 350
Now led by Fancy's visionary ray,
She soars unfetter'd through th' aërial way.

* See letters on different subjects by the Author of " The Unfortunate Mo-
" ther's Advice to her absent Daughters." (Lady *Pennington*.)

The tender mind form'd by her fost'ring hand,
It's weak ideas quickly learns t'expand:
'Tis Hers to charm in ev'ry varied scene,   355
Though witty modest, and though warm serene.

Say Montagu * can this unartful verse
Thy Genius, Learning, or thy Worth rehearse?
To paint thy talents justly should conspire
Thy taste, thy judgment, and thy Shakespeare's fire. 360
Well hath thy Pen with nice discernment trac'd
What various pow'rs the Matchless Poet grac'd;
Well hath thy Pen his various beauties shown,
And prov'd thy soul congenial to his own.
Charm'd with those splendid honours of thy Name, 365
Fain would the Muse relate thy nobler Fame;

* Mrs. *Montagu*, Author of the " Essay on the Genius and Writings of
" Shakespeare, compared with the Greek and French Dramatic Poets."

Dear

Dear to Religion, as to Learning dear,
Candid, obliging, modest, mild, sincere,
Still prone to soften at another's woe,
Still fond to bless, still ready to bestow. 370

O, sweet Philanthropy! thou guest divine!
What permanent, what heart-felt joys are thine!
Supremely blest the maid, whose generous soul
Bends all-obedient to thy soft controul:
Nature's vast theatre her eye surveys, 375
Studious to trace Eternal Wisdom's ways;
Marks what dependencies, what different ties,
Throughout the spacious scale of beings rise;
Sees Providence's oft-mysterious plan,
Form'd to promote the general good of man. 380
With noble warmth thence her expanded mind
Feels for the welfare of all human-kind:
Thence flows each lenient art that sooths distress,
And thence the unremitting wish to bless!

Th' aspiring Muse now droops her trembling wings, 385
Whilst, INDOLENCE, * thy tranquil pow'r she sings;
"Not sordid sloth," the low-born mind's disease,
But calm retirement, and poetic ease.
Ah! let me ever live with THEE immur'd,
From Folly's laugh, from envy's rage secur'd, 390
In ev'ry scene of changeful life the same,
Not fondly courting, nor despising Fame.

TALBOT, ‡ did e'er mortality enshrine
A mind more gen'rous, meek, or kind, than thine?
Delightful moralist! thy well-wrote page 395
Shall please, correct, and mend the rising age;

Point

See *Indolence* a Poem, by the Author of *Almida* a Tragedy. (Mrs. *Celesia*, daughter of the late Mr. *Mallett*.)

‡ Mrs. *Catherine Talbot*, only daughter of the Reverend *Edward Talbot*, Archdeacon of *Berks*, and Preacher at the *Rolls*; (younger son of Dr. *Talbot* Bishop of *Durham*.) This truly excellent Lady was blest with the happiest natural talents: her understanding was vigorous, her imagination lively, and

the

Point out the road the thoughtlefs many mifs,
That leads through virtue to the realms of blifs.
Fain would my foul thy fentiments imbibe,
And fain thy manners in my own tranfcribe : 400
Genius and Wit were but thy fecond praife,
Thou knew'ft to win by ftill fublimer ways;
Thy Angel-goodnefs, all who knew approv'd,
Honour'd, admir'd, applauded too, and lov'd!
Fair fhall thy fame to lateft ages bloom, 405
And ev'ry Mufe with tears bedew thy tomb.

And THOU † whofe pen, congenial to thy breaft,
Hath fhown us Virtue by the Graces dreft;

her tafte refined. Her virtues were equal to her genius, and rendered her at once the object of univerfal love and admiration. She was the Author of "Reflections on the Seven Days of the Week;" and of "Effays on various Sub-jects," 2 volumes. Her writings breathe the nobleft fpirit of Chriftian benevolence; and difcover a more than common acquaintance with human nature.

† See " Sermons by *A Lady*, The Tranflatrefs of four felect Tales from " *Marmontel*."

Hath ſtigmatiz'd the miſer's narrow aim,
And bid our youth revere a parent's claim; 410
Taught us that nought beneath yon radiant ſky,
The mind's unbounded wiſhes can ſupply;
Still in the glorious race, O let thy ſoul
Preſs boldly on, Eternal Life's the goal!

Nor ſhalt THOU † be forgot whoſe tuneful tongue 415
So well the charms of STRAWBERRY-HILL hath ſung;
Long ſhall thy wit in WALPOLE's numbers live,
When dead the little honours mine can give.

Fir'd with the Muſic, AIKIN, ‡ of thy lays,
To thee the Muſe a joyful tribute pays; 420

† See Poems by *A Lady*, printed for *Walter* in 1771.
‡ See Poems and Miſcellaneous Pieces in Proſe, by Miſs *Aikin*, (daughter of the Reverend Mr. Aikin, one of the tutors to the Academy at Warrington) lately married to the Reverend Mr. Rochemont Barbauld.

Tranſported

Transported dwells on that harmonious line,
Where taste, and spirit, wit, and learning shine;
Where Fancy's hand her richest colourings lends,
And ev'ry shade in just proportion blends.
How fair, how beauteous to our gazing eyes   425
Thy vivid intellectual paintings rise!
We feel thy feelings, glow with all thy fires,
Adopt thy thoughts, and pant with thy desires.
Proceed, bright maid! and may thy polish'd page
Refine the manners of a trifling age: 430
Thy sex apprize of pleasure's treach'rous charms,
And woo them from the Syren's fatal arms;
Teach them with thee on Fancy's wing to soar,
With thee, the paths of science to explore;
With thee, the open book of Nature scan,   435
Yet nobly scorn the little pride of Man.

Man, seated high on Learning's awful throne,
Thinks the fair realms of knowledge his alone;
But you, ye fair, his Salic Law disclaim:
Supreme in Science shall the Tyrant reign!   440
When every talent all-indulgent Heav'n
In lavish bounty to your share hath giv'n?

With joy ineffable the Muse surveys
The orient beams of more resplendent days:
As on she raptur'd looks to future years,   445
What a bright throng to Fancy's view appears!
To them see Genius her best gifts impart,
And Science raise a throne in ev'ry heart!
One turns the moral, one th' historic page;
Another glows with all a SHAKESPEARE's rage!   450
With matchless NEWTON now one soars on high,
Lost in the boundless wonders of the sky;
Another now, of curious mind, reveals
What treasures in her bowels Earth conceals;

Nature's minuter works attract her eyes;   455
Their laws, their pow'rs, her deep research descries.
From sense abstracted, some, with arduous flight,
Explore the realms of intellectual light;
With unremitting study seek to find,
How mind on matter, matter acts on mind: 460
Alike in nature, arts, and manners read,
In ev'ry path of knowledge, see they tread!
Whilst men, convinc'd of Female Talents, pay
To Female Worth the tributary lay.

 Yet now there sure are some of nobler kind,   465
From all their sex's narrow views refin'd,
Who, truly wise, attempt not to controul
The generous ardor of th' aspiring soul:
Such, tuneful DUNCOMBE,* thou, whose Attic lays
Demand the warmest strains of grateful praise: 470

 * The Reverend *John Duncombe* M. A. Fellow of Corpus Christi College *Cambridge*, Rector of St. Andrew's and St. Mary Bredman's, one of the Six Preachers at the Cathedral at Canterbury, and Author of the *Feminead*, or
              Female

Fearless of censure, boldly thou stood'st forth
An able Advocate for Female Worth!
For that! may the far-sounding Voice of Fame,
To latest Ages bear thy honour'd Name;
For that! may Fancy still her aid impart, 475
And still the Muse's smile dilate thy heart;
For that! may Hope still strew thy path with flow'rs,
And ev'ry blessing crown thy circling hours!

Such HE † who dared " against a World decide,
" And stem the rage of Custom's rapid tide;" 480

Female Genius, A Poem. " The Ladies there celebrated are Mrs. *Catherine Philips*, *Anne* Countess of *Winchelsea*, Mrs. *Cockburn*, Mrs. *Rowe*, *Frances* Dutchess Dowager of *Somerset*, *Anne* Viscountess *Irwin*, Mrs. *Wright*, Mrs. *Madan*, Mrs. *Leapor*, Mrs. *Carter*, Mrs. *Brooke*, Miss *Ferrar*, (now Mrs. *Peckard*); Miss *Pennington*, (since dead); Miss *Mulso*, (now Mrs. *Chapone*); and Miss *Highmore* (since married to the Author)."

† See a Poem in *Dodsley's* Miscellanies, intituled, " The Female Right to " Literature, in a Letter to a Young Lady from *Florence*," written by the Reverend Mr. *Seward*, Canon of *Litchfield*.

Who kindly bade ATHENIA's " growing mind,
" Take ev'ry knowledge in of ev'ry kind."

And fuch art THOU, my ever-valued friend;
Ah! ftill thy candour to the Mufe extend.:
Permit that honour'd Name to grace her page,   485
Which fhames the manners of a felfifh age!
(That name, whofe merit ftill this heart muft feel,
Yet vainly ftrive that merit to reveal!)
✗ PHILANDER! generous, affable, fincere,
His tafte as polifh'd as his judgment clear,   490
Bleft with the tendereft feelings of the Heart,
Wife without Stiffnefs, prudent without Art,
Form'd with like eafe t' enjoy a profp'rous ftate
Or bear the ftorms of unpropitious fate.

Such HE, who, when I firft attun'd the lay,   495.
With his own candour view'd the faint effay;

En-

Enjoin'd me still to court the Muse's smile,
The tiresome hours of languor to beguile.
O could this pen, which gratitude impells,
But tell how ——— in each scene excels! 500
O could she but some glowing colours find,
To paint each feature of his finish'd mind!
A mind, unstain'd with vanity, or art,
The gentlest manners, and the kindest heart!
A mind where prudence, judgement, taste unite, 505
Though learn'd yet humble, though sincere polite;
His passions calm'd, his wishes all subdu'd,
But these (the noblest!) to be wise and good.

   Ye generous pleaders of the female cause,
Ye friends to Nature's (her's are Reason's laws) 510
For you the Muse shall raise her drooping wing,
And Peans echo from each trembling string.

Though

[handwritten annotation: a well known physician who lives at Blandford]

Though funk with languor, and unceafing pains,
Life's purple current ftagnates in my veins;
Though Fancy mourns her fairy vifions fled,   515
And all the fond, fond hopes of youth are dead!
Still next to virtue, fcience charms my eye,
And frequent prompts the unavailing figh.

But O would Heav'n my faded health renew,
Unwearied I'd the glorious toils purfue;   520
Well-pleas'd in fweet retirement's fhady bow'rs,
In ftudious eafe, to fpend my remnant hours.

F I N I S.

Juſt Publiſhed,

Printed for J. JOHNSON, No. 72, St. Paul's Church-Yard.

I. Poems, by Miſs A. L. Aikin, (now Mrs. Barbauld) fourth edition, price 3s. ſewed.

II. Miſcellaneous Pieces in Proſe. By J. and A. L. Aikin, price 3s. ſewed.

III. Eſſays on Song-Writing, with a Collection of ſuch Engliſh Songs as are moſt eminent for poetical Merit. By J. Aikin, 3s. 6d. ſewed.

N. B. The above Three Volumes may be had, *uniformly bound*, price 12s.

IV. The Matron, an Elegy, price 6d.

V. Letters by ſeveral eminent Perſons deceaſed; including the Correſpondence of John Hughes, Eſq. (Author of the Siege of Damaſcus) and ſeveral of his Friends, viz. Lord Chancellor Cowper, Biſhop Hoadly, Lord Chief Baron Gilbert, Mr. Addiſon, Sir Richard Steele, Sir Godfrey Kneller, Dr. Watts, Mr. Pope, Mr. Rowe, Mr. Robert Wilks, &c. &c. And to this Edition are added ſeveral by Archbiſhop Herring, the Earl of Corke, the Counteſſes of Pomfret and Hertford, Biſhops Benſon and Rundle, Dean Swift, Mr. Pitt, Mr. Dyer, Mr. Spence, Mr. S. Richardſon, Mrs. Rowe, &c. &c. Publiſhed from the Originals, with Notes explanatory and hiſtorical. By John Duncombe, M. A. 3 vol. ſecond edition, greatly enlarged, price 9s. ſewed.

N. B. All the Additions to this Edition are printed in a ſeparate Volume (price 3s. ſewed) in order to complete the firſt Edition.

VI. Letters Religious and Moral, deſigned particularly for the Entertainment of young Perſons. By *Daniel Turner*, A. M. price 3s. *bound*.

VII. Another Traveller! or, curſory Remarks and critical Obſervations made upon a Journey through Part of the Netherlands in the latter End of the Year, 1766. By Corial Junior, 3 vols. 9s. *bound*.

VIII. Joineriana; or, the Book of Scraps, under the following Heads, viz.

ANTIQUARY,	FOLLY,	FAIRS AND WAKES,
AUTHOR,	FREETHINKER,	SLEEP,
BOOKMAKER,	LAW AND LAWYERS,	THEATRE,
BOOKS,	LITERARY PROPERTY,	TRISTRAM SHANDY,
BOOKSELLER,	MELANCHOLY,	WANT,
COWLEY,	MERIT,	WISDOM,
DEDICATION,	NEWS & NEWSWRITERS,	VANITY.
EPITAPH,	ORATORS & ORATORY,	2 Vols. price 5s. ſewed.

IX. Peregrinations of the Mind through the moſt general and intereſting Subjects which are uſually agitated in Life. By the Rationaliſt. price 3s. *bound*.

X. Voltaire in the Shades; or, Dialogues on the Deiſtical Controverſy, price 3s. *bound*.

XI. Obſervations on Literary Property. By W. Enfield, L. L. D. 2s.